Body Language

KAREN PRICE HOSSELL

Heinemann Library
Chicago, Illinois

© 2002 Heinemann Library
a division of Reed Elsevier Inc.
Chicago, Illinois

Customer Service 888-454-2279

Visit our website at www.heinemannlibrary.com

All rights reserved. No part of this publication may be reproduced or transmitted in any form or by any means, electronic or mechanical, including photocopying, recording, taping, or any information storage and retrieval system, without permission in writing from the publisher.

Page Layout by Vicki Fischman
Photo research by Amor Montes de Oca
Printed and bound in the United States by
Lake Book Manufacturing, Inc.

07 06 05 04
10 9 8 7 6 5 4 3 2

Library of Congress Cataloging-in-Publication Data
Price Hossell, Karen, 1957-
   Body language / Karen Price Hossell.
      p. cm. -- (Communicating)
Summary: Presents an overview of the types, functions, and meanings of body language, how it is used by people in different professions, and some of the differences in interpreting body language in other countries and cultures. Includes bibliographical references and index.
   ISBN 1-58810-483-4 (HC), 1-58810-939-9 (Pbk.)
   1. Body language--Juvenile literature. [1. Body language.] I. Title.
II. Series.
BF637.N66 .P74 2002
302.2'22--dc21
                              2002001689

Acknowledgments
The author and publishers are grateful to the following for permission to reproduce copyright material:
Cover photography by (TL) Janette Beckman/Corbis; (BL) Kevin R. Morris/Corbis; (R) Francine Fleischer/Corbis, p. 2 Kevin R. Morris/Corbis; pp. 3, 45C Brian Warling/Heinemann Library; p. 4T EyeWire; pp. 4B, 6C, 13R, 18, 19 Mark Downey; p. 5 Tom McCarthy/Unicorn Stock Photos; pp. 6T, 37T Jack McConnell; pp. 6B, 33, 37B Michael Newman/PhotoEdit, Inc; pp. 8, 20T, 22T, 24 Jeff Greenberg/Visuals Unlimited; pp. 9, 23T Victor Englebert; p. 10T Jim Brandenburg/Minden Pictures; p. 10C Elyse Lewin/The Image Bank/Getty Images; pp. 10B, 11TR Frans Lanting/Minden Pictures; pp. 11TL, 34BR H. Rogers/Trip; p. 11B Bettmann/Corbis; pp. 12, 16B, 21BR, 23B, 26, 30T, 34T, 34BL, 38B, 39B, 42, 43, 45 Robert Lifson/Heinemann Library; pp. 13L, 20B Mary Kate Denny/PhotoEdit, Inc.; p. 14 Tony Freeman/PhotoEdit, Inc.; p. 15 Jim Arbogast/Getty Images; pp. 16T, 35, 38T David Young-Wolff/PhotoEdit, Inc.; p. 17 Novastock/Unicorn Stock Photos; p. 21L John Boykin/PhotoEdit, Inc.; p. 21TR S. Grant/Trip; p. 22C Robert Brenner/PhotoEdit, Inc.; p. 22B A. Gurmankin & M. Morina/Visuals Unlimited; p. 25 Gary A. Conner/PhotoEdit, Inc.; p. 27 Richard T. Nowitz; p. 28T Trineete Reed/Corbis; p. 28B David Woods/Corbis; p. 29 Laura Zito; p. 30B T. Freeman/Trip; p. 32B SW Productions/PhotoDisc; p. 36L Konrad Wothe/Minden Pictures; p. 36TR Nancy Sheehan/PhotoEdit, Inc.; p. 36CR Linda H. Hopson/Visuals Unlimited; p. 36BR Cheryl A. Ertelt/Visuals Unlimited; p. 39T Roger Wood/Corbis; p. 39C Gary W. Carter/Visuals Unlimited; p. 40B Sergio Dorantes/Corbis; p. 41 Dennis MacDonald.

Every effort has been made to contact copyright holders of any material reproduced in this book. Any omissions will be rectified in subsequent printings if notice is given to the publisher.

Some words are shown in bold, **like this.** You can find out what they mean by looking in the glossary.

Contents

Communication Is More Than Words 4
The Signs of the Eyes and Eyebrows 6
Eye Contact 8
The Mouth Isn't Just for Talking .10
Posture 12
Personal Distance 14
The Hands Speak 16
The Voice 18
Gestures 20
Touch 22
Speaking and Listening 24
You Can't Help It! 26
Happy and Sad 28
Fear and Relaxation 30
Disgust and Surprise 32
Your Emotions Are Showing! 34
Animals and Body Language 36
Body Language and Gestures Around the World 38
Careers and Body Language 40
Appendix A: Common Emotions and Body Language Signs . .42
Appendix B: Common Gestures 44
More Books to Read 45
Glossary 46
Index 48

Communication Is More Than Words

What do you do when you want to communicate something? Usually, you speak. You take a second to think about what words you want to use. Then you open your mouth and say them.

Words are important. They help us to communicate our thoughts, our feelings, and our needs. We use words to express ourselves all the time. But there is something else we use to show how we feel. It is called **body language.** We use our faces and body movements to communicate with others. The study of body language is called **kinesics.** People who study body language are called **behaviorists.** They study the way people behave.

We use body language when we are speaking and when we are not speaking. This kind of communication is also called **nonverbal communication.** That means that we are not using words to communicate. Instead, we use smiles, groans, head shakes, and more.

We cannot hear what these girls are saying, but their body language tells us a lot about their conversation. The girl on the right is excited about something, while the girl on the left may not be so interested.

Your body language can show if you are paying attention. This girl is obviously bored, but the boy is paying attention to what is going on in the class.

Think about when you are sitting in your classroom, listening to your teacher. What do you do while your teacher speaks? Do you sit quietly with your hands folded on your desk? Do you look around the room, or do you look at the teacher? Do you rest your head on your hand and yawn? Do you fiddle with your pencil?

These are all different kinds of body language. You show your teachers what you think of what they are saying by the way you **react.** If you look directly at a teacher while he or she is speaking, the teacher will think you are paying attention. If you look around the room or rest your head on your hand, your teacher will probably think you are bored. Your teachers look for these signals to know how well their students are learning.

Body language is made up of hundreds of signals. The more you know about body language, the better you will be able to understand people. You will find out that people do not always say what they mean. Many times, their body language says it for them—even if they do not realize it. If you are paying attention, you can pick up many clues to how people are thinking and feeling just by observing their body language!

Know It

Behaviorists say that more than half of human communication is nonverbal.

The Signs of the Eyes and Eyebrows

One of the most important ways we can send signals without speaking is with our eyes. Eyes do more than just see—they express our feelings and **reactions** as well. When you look at the pictures of eyes on this page, you can probably tell how the people in the pictures feel. You can do this without hearing them talk or seeing any other part of their bodies. That is because the eyes are very **expressive**. For example, eyes that are wide open can show fear. People often squint their eyes when they are **suspicious** or when they are confused.

The eyes can show other **emotions**, too. A happy person's eyes may be bright and cheerful—sometimes they almost seem to sparkle. Someone who is sad may look down and have tears in their eyes. People often wipe or rub their eyes or try to blink back the tears when they are crying. A wink—closing just one eye—can appear playful, or it can mean that the person is sharing a secret. A person who rolls his or her eyes may be showing amazement, disbelief, or frustration.

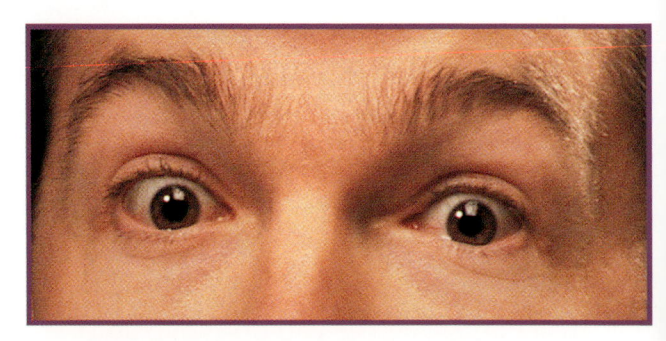

Wide-open eyes and raised eyebrows show that a person is surprised.

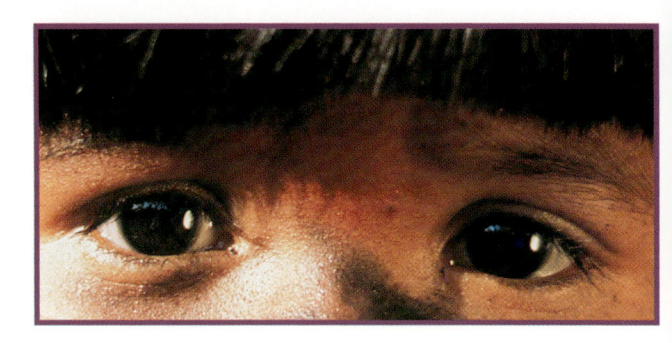

This girl's eyes are watery with tears. She is probably sad.

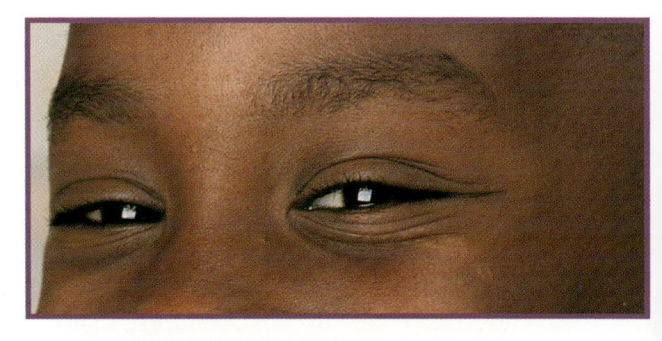

These eyes show happiness. They are bright and cheerful, and they even sparkle.

The eyebrows play an important part in eye communication, too. People move their eyebrows up and down all the time, especially when speaking and listening. They do not usually realize they are doing it. They use their eyebrows to send signals. Raised eyebrows, for example, often mean that someone is surprised or that they do not believe what someone else is saying. Lowered eyebrows can show doubt or disagreement. They can also show that someone is concentrating hard.

> ### Try this
> Stand in front of a mirror and try these exercises. You may not be able to do some of them—you may not be able to do any of them—but it is fun to try.
> - Can you raise just one eyebrow?
> - Can you wiggle your ears?
> - Can you smile with your mouth and frown with your eyes and eyebrows? What happens when you try? Most people end up frowning with their mouths when they try to frown with their eyes.
> - How long can you hold a smile? People who need to smile all the time, such as television **anchors** and beauty pageant contestants, say their faces ache after a long day of smiling!

Have you ever had a parent or teacher look at you with his or her eyebrows close together? That person may have been glaring at you with angry or upset eyes as well. He or she was probably sending you a signal of disapproval or telling you to "cut it out." People's eyebrows also move when they are happy, and they can even communicate friendship and love. For example, when people greet each other, their eyebrows often raise quickly and then return to their normal position. This movement is called an eyebrow "flash," and it is usually accompanied by a smile. The eyebrow flash is used as part of friendly greetings in **cultures** all around the world. No matter where you travel, people who do not speak your language will recognize your greeting. They will probably even smile back.

Eye Contact

One important part of **nonverbal communication** is **eye contact**, or looking directly into a person's eyes. Eye contact is often a way to show interest in someone or something. When people talk, they often look into each other's eyes, but usually not for long periods of time. If people know each other well, they may hold eye contact longer. For example, when you talk to your best friend, you probably look into his or her eyes longer than you would look into a stranger's eyes. People who are in love often gaze into each other's eyes for a long time.

Eye contact can tell you a lot about people. People who make eye contact most of the time are seen as honest and trustworthy. They usually have **confidence** in themselves and in what they are saying. People who do not look into another person's eyes when they are speaking are considered to be dishonest or hiding something. It is not always fair to think that, though. Sometimes people do not

When people are sad, they usually look down and avoid eye contact.

People who are ashamed of something will look down and not at other people.

To gain respect, people who are in charge will keep their eyes on the person they are speaking to.

like to look directly at other people because they are shy. They simply do not feel comfortable making steady eye contact with others. People who are very sad tend to look down or away from other people. People who feel ashamed do this, too. They may be afraid that making eye contact will reveal what they have done wrong.

This is also true of people who are lying about something. They may look away from others to hide their guilt. However, if they are used to lying, they may also look directly into a person's eyes to try to make themselves appear truthful. This can make it harder for others to know whether or not to believe what the person is saying. People who want to show that they are in charge will usually hold eye contact more often than the people they are speaking to. It is seen as a way of getting respect. This is why teachers and parents often say, "Look at me when I am talking to you!"

Know It

People looking at photographs almost always look at the eyes of the photographed people first. This can help them to get a feeling for the person's mood when the picture was taken.

The Mouth Isn't Just for Talking

You use your mouth to speak words every day. But your mouth can also communicate without saying anything. A smile can often mean more than words. So can a frown. A mouth open in horror or surprise says just as much as words can, or even more.

When people are happy, they smile. But there are many different kinds of smiles. A small smile might show that a person is feeling relaxed or comfortable. A medium smile could mean that a person thinks something is funny, but not too funny. A big smile usually means that a person is very happy.

Sometimes people smile even when they are not happy. Smiles are easy to control, so they can be put on as "masks" to cover up worry, fear, uncertainty, or unhappiness. This is especially true in some **cultures** that expect people to control their **emotions** in public. Some smiles let sadness or fear show through. They let others know that although the

This is a very small, relaxed smile.

This medium smile could show wonder.

A big smile indicates true happiness.

10

Sometimes people use fake smiles—they don't really want to smile, but they do anyway. Some people are good at these kinds of smiles, but others are not. The sides of their mouths look strained.

person wearing the smile is not in the best mood, he or she will try to "put on a happy face." Sometimes cruel people smile when they get their way, no matter who else gets hurt. That unpleasant kind of smile looks much different from a happy smile. You can probably think of many more kinds of smiles. **Behaviorists** say there are at least 50 different smiles!

When people are really happy, their whole face smiles. The smile shows in the eyes as well as in the mouth. When reading a person's **facial expression,** you often have to look at the whole face, not just part of it.

Mona Lisa

Mona Lisa is a famous painting by the Italian artist Leonardo da Vinci. One reason the painting is so well known is because of *Mona Lisa's* smile. It has inspired many people to wonder who the model for the painting was. Some have proposed that she was a wealthy lady of Florence, Italy, where da Vinci lived. Others have said da Vinci was actually painting his own face. Whatever the case, people have called the smile mysterious, haunting, and timeless. What is it about *Mona Lisa's* smile that makes them say this?

11

Posture

Posture, or the way a person stands or sits, is a kind of **body language.** Posture shows how much you are interested in people and what they are saying. It can show how much you like or dislike someone, or whether you agree or disagree with someone. It can even show who is in charge in a situation.

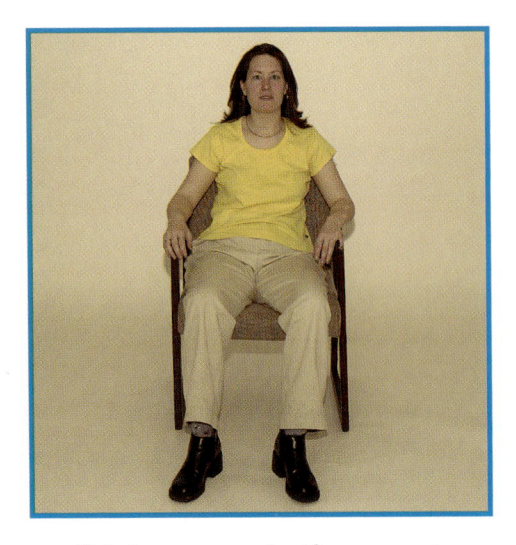

People who study body language often talk about two main kinds of posture: open and closed. Open posture is when a person stands or sits in a relaxed position, with the arms unfolded and hands open or loosely held together. A person with open posture faces the speaker and often leans forward toward him or her. This posture usually shows agreement with the speaker or comfort with the situation. People who cross their arms across their chests, cross their legs, and turn their bodies away from a speaker are said to have closed posture. That kind of posture usually shows disagreement with what the speaker is saying or discomfort with the situation.

People who are interested in what a speaker has to say will sit up straight. They may lean forward a little and tuck their legs back under the chair. On the other hand, a person who is bored may lean back in their chair and rest their head on one hand. They stretch their legs out in front of them and look at the ceiling or out of the window. They may look at their watch a lot, yawn, or fiddle

This is an example of open posture. The woman is probably interested in what is being said.

Closed posture shows that a person disagrees or feels uncomfortable.

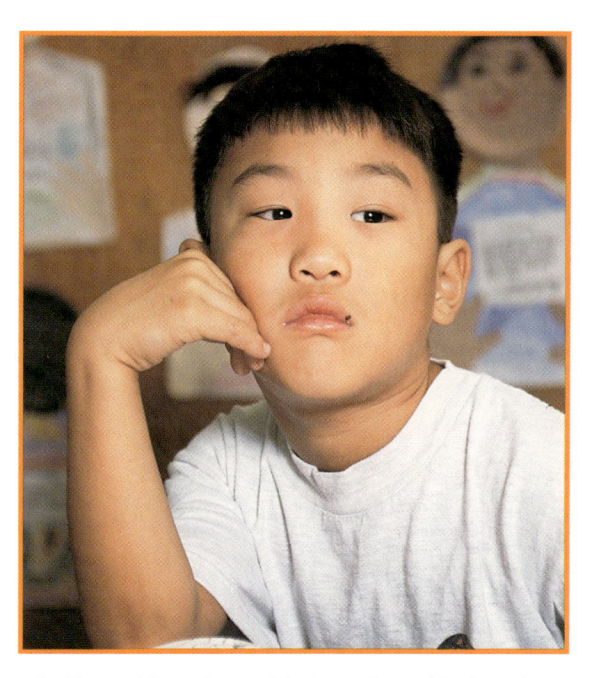

Everything about this boy, from his head resting on his hand to his distracted eyes, shows that he is bored.

People lean away from strangers, someone they disagree with, or someone they do not like. They lean toward someone they like or agree with.

with something, such as a pencil. Bored people may also doodle on paper. Sometimes people become so bored when listening to a speaker that they fall asleep!

People who are in charge of a situation can show their **authority** by their posture. Teachers, leaders, bosses, and other authority figures usually stand straight and tall to show that they are in command of what is happening. They look alert and ready for anything.

Your posture can be related to your **emotions,** too. People who are happy and excited may stand up tall. They may even jump and wave their arms. People who are sad, scared, or in danger often try to make themselves small by ducking their heads, slumping, kneeling, or even curling up into a ball. In addition, watching a suspenseful movie can truly keep people "on the edge of their seats."

Know It

People in charge may make **gestures** such as pointing and putting their hands on their hips to "show others who's boss."

Personal Distance

Have you ever felt uncomfortable when someone stands next to you because he or she is standing too close? The reason you feel uncomfortable is that the person has **violated** your sense of personal distance. We feel most comfortable when we stand or sit a certain distance from one another.

You can test this by getting one or two friends and doing an **experiment.** Pretend that you and your friends are standing in the hallway of your school and talking. Stand the way you normally would. Then start moving closer to your friends. Tell them to let you know when you have gotten too close.

They probably thought you were too close when you got closer than about eighteen inches (46 centimeters). Good friends can stand or sit about eighteen inches from each other. Anything closer than that makes most people feel uncomfortable. If you are talking to someone you do not know very well, you probably want that person to stay eighteen inches to four feet (one meter) away. This is true for most people in the United States and countries in northern Europe, such as Great Britain. In some other **cultures,** people are more comfortable when someone stands closer to them.

You have probably seen many examples of personal distance. When people go into a movie theater or waiting room, for example, they almost always put an empty seat between themselves and a stranger, unless the room is very crowded. When people

When people stand in line, they usually try to put an equal amount of space in front of them and behind them.

14

go to the beach, they always put a certain distance between their towel or blanket and the people nearby. When someone sits on a park bench next to a stranger, they leave at least eighteen inches between them and the stranger. In an elevator, people arrange themselves so that they are all about an equal distance away from strangers. However, friends or family members on elevators usually stand a little closer to one another.

When people are forced to sit next to strangers, they often put up **barriers** between themselves and the strangers. For example, a woman sitting on a park bench may put a bag or newspaper on the bench between herself and a stranger. In a crowded waiting room, on an airplane, or on a train, people will read or listen to music through headphones as a kind of barrier between themselves and the people around them. People will also stand or sit turned away from strangers.

> **Know It**
>
> The study of personal distance is called **proxemics.**

In this waiting room, the distance between each person is much less than eighteen inches. Most of the people here have put up barriers to distract themselves.

15

The Hands Speak

As she speaks, this girl is making a hand **gesture** with her palm facing up. This shows that she is being open with the other girl.

The man speaking on the right has his hand behind his head. He may not be entirely sure about what he is saying. The listener could have a hard time believing him after seeing this **body language**.

Do you use your hands when you talk? Almost everyone does. Some people use their hands a lot, and others rarely do. You can test how often you do by asking your friends. An even better way to test yourself is to try not to use your hands the next time you talk for a long period of time. Can you do it?

People use their hands when they talk to help others understand what they are trying to say. Some things are hard to put into words, so we move our hands in certain ways to help us explain. Hand movements like these are called **illustrators,** because they help to illustrate our speech, just like a picture helps to illustrate a story in a book.

We communicate with our hands in other ways, too. In fact, our hands rarely stop moving. When you get a chance, look at the hands of people around you. Few people sit or stand for long without moving their hands.

The position of our hands can show how we feel. When people put their hands behind their heads, it can show that they are not sure about what is being said. It could also show that they are not very sure about what they themselves are saying. It can mean that they feel anger, frustration, or disagreement. If someone feels one of these **emotions** strongly, they may rub or scratch the back of their neck.

When people put their hands on their hips, they may be showing that they are ready to take charge or do something, and that they feel **confident** about it. People also put their hands on their hips when they are bothered by something or when they are angry.

Other hand positions that communicate messages involve turning the palms up or down. When someone stands or sits with their palms down, it is seen as being "closed" or maybe even unfriendly. The "palms down" position can also show that they are in charge and feel confident. When people sit or stand with their palms up, they are seen as more open and friendly. However, when people shrug their shoulders to show they don't know something, they often hold up their hands with their palms facing up. So, having palms facing up can also be a sign of doubt or confusion.

The handshake

People in many parts of the world greet one another with a handshake. In the United States and Great Britain, men and women both use the handshake as a form of greeting, but men often do it more than women. The handshake is an important gesture. People prefer to shake hands with someone who has a strong handshake, and some people even judge others by how they shake hands. People whose handshakes are weak may be seen as weak themselves. Some people shake hands and use their free hand to grasp the other person's arm. Other times, people may grab a person's hand with both of their own. Some people see this as a form of control, although it could also be seen as warm and protective.

The Voice

It may seem odd to include the voice in a book about **body language** and **nonverbal communication**. That's because we use our voices when we are **verbal**—when we talk. There is more to voice, though, than just the words we say. One kind of body language has to do with how we use our voices.

Have you ever heard someone say, "It's not what you said, it's the way you said it"? They are talking about the body language behind voice, or the way we use our voices when we speak. Besides the meaning of the words we speak, our voices communicate messages through their **pitch, tone, volume**, and **pace**.

This woman's voice probably has an angry tone with a high pitch, loud volume, and fast pace. Together with the words she is speaking, these voice qualities communicate her feelings very effectively.

Pitch is the highness or lowness of a voice. Each person's voice has a regular pitch for everyday conversation. But sometimes when people get excited or angry, their voices go up in pitch, and they may sound like they are **shrieking**. The voice also has a variety of tones—the feelings behind our words. A voice can have a loving tone, a cruel tone, or many other tones, depending on the feelings of the speaker.

Another voice quality includes volume, which is the loudness or softness of a voice. A loud voice often brings a message of anger, excitement, or urgency. A softer or quieter voice can be more gentle and loving. Finally, pace is the speed at which someone speaks.

Some people naturally speak faster or slower than others. However, people who are excited or nervous may speak more quickly, while those who are calm and relaxed may speak more slowly.

The way we say things—including the pitch, tone, volume, and pace we use—can say as much as or more than the words we use. The different qualities of our voices combine with the words we speak to communicate our message more completely. These qualities can help people understand what we mean. They can also affect the way people respond to us. People can tell from our voices whether we are angry, friendly, or nervous, and they will respond to us accordingly.

To see more clearly how changes in voice can affect your message, choose a sentence like "I can't believe what you just did." Try saying it several times in different ways. Each time, change your pitch, tone, volume, or pace. Do you sound excited? Angry? How else can the sentence sound?

You can see that the same words spoken differently can mean different things. For a message to be clear, it is important to check that your spoken words, voice qualities, and any other body language are all in agreement. If not, your listeners could be confused.

A mother uses gentle words to relax her baby. She combines these words with a soothing tone of voice, low pitch, soft volume, and slow pace.

19

Gestures

Gestures are special **nonverbal** signs that are understood by many people. Different gestures are used throughout the world. **Behaviorists** have recorded at least 700,000 different gestures.

Some of the most common gestures used in the United States are the handshake, head nodding and shaking, waving hello and goodbye, and using the fingers or hands to call someone over. When we use these forms of **body language,** most of the people around us—the people in our **culture**—understand what they mean.

That may not be true in other parts of the world, however. For example, in most countries, shaking your head from side to side means "no." In Ethiopia, though, people do not shake their heads from side to side to mean "no." Instead, they turn their heads to one side and then back to the normal position.

There are other examples of cultural differences, too. In most of the world, people wave hello or goodbye with their palms facing outward. But in Italy, people wave with their palms toward their bodies. British **royalty** will wave this way, too, when on **official business.** In many parts of the world, the sign for "Be quiet!" is made

Hand clapping is a gesture usually made in large groups to show appreciation for a good performance.

When people yawn, they are probably bored or tired.

20

Many people understand this gesture to mean "everything is okay." But in Japan, it also means "five."

In Italy, this gesture indicates boredom.

Raised fists are usually a sign for victory.

by putting the index finger against the lips. In Saudi Arabia, though, people make that same motion and then blow on their finger to tell someone to be quiet.

Many other gestures are made in only one country. For example, in the Netherlands, when people want to make a sign that means "I swear it is true," they touch the tips of their index and middle fingers to their eyes. In Japan, people put a flat hand in front of the face to show that they are apologizing. In France, people slide an index finger under the nose to mean "too late."

Because people of different countries recognize different gestures, it is important to be careful about the gestures you make. **Diplomats** and world leaders are sometimes embarrassed to discover that gestures they thought would be **universally** understood actually mean something different—even negative or offensive—in the countries they are visiting.

Know It

Even simple gestures like "thumbs up" and showing an open hand with the palm facing out are considered rude and insulting in some other cultures.

Touch

One kind of **body language** is touch. Touch can show people that we care for them and support them. It can also show people that we appreciate them. Sometimes people touch others to get their attention or to show them the way, such as when someone touches a person's shoulder to let him or her know which way to turn.

Society has rules, though, about touching. When we touch strangers by mistake, such as when we bump into them or have to brush by them in crowded places, we often say "Excuse me." Usually the only time we can politely touch strangers is when we tap them on the shoulder to get their attention.

In some **cultures,** people touch more often. **Behaviorists** call these contact cultures. In one study, behaviorists studied people in Puerto Rico, France, the United States, and England. In Puerto Rico, pairs of people touched about 180 times an hour. Pairs of people in France touched about 110 times in an hour. In the United States, people touched fewer than two times an hour, and in England they didn't

In some cultures, people stand close to one another when talking and sometimes touch each other as they speak.

Most people don't mind when a close family member or good friend touches their hair. But this is a "no-touch" zone when it comes to strangers, unless the stranger is cutting your hair.

Hugs from close family members can make us feel safe and loved.

22

When we are packed close together, we usually excuse strangers for bumping into us.

touch at all. When people from these different cultures come together, they can have misunderstandings if they do not realize that cultures have different rules and expectations about touching while having a conversation.

The kinds of touch people make when talking include touching someone's hand and arm, touching hair, and putting a hand on someone's back. The better we know people, the more comfortable we are with touching and being touched by them. When strangers touch us in these ways, though, we usually feel uncomfortable. It is always okay to maintain your personal distance with people you do not know well.

Sometimes touching takes the place of words. If someone we care about feels really bad, we may not be able to think of anything to say. But if we touch that person's hand or give a hug, it may make them feel better.

Keep your hands to yourself

How long can you sit before you touch yourself in some way? Everyone does it—it is almost impossible not to. We rub our hands together, fold our arms, cross our legs, or touch our fingers. We pull on our hair, rub our eyes, and brush our fingers across our lips.

Behaviorists think people touch themselves in these ways to relieve **tension** and **anxiety.** It is like we are telling ourselves that everything is all right.

23

Speaking and Listening

The ability to read **body language** is always important, but it really helps us to understand other people when we are speaking and listening. When people are having a conversation, they pay attention to the **nonverbal** signals others send. These signals show if someone is listening or if they are finished speaking. The speaker usually looks more at the listener than the listener looks at the speaker. The listener will look at the speaker for a second or two, then glance away. However, speakers do not watch listeners the entire time they are speaking. They start out by looking at the listener and begin to speak. After a second or two, they look away. When they are finished speaking, they look back at the listener to let him or her know they are finished. When the people who are talking like each other, they look at each other more. If they do not like each other or if they disagree, they will usually look away more.

Speakers look at listeners to make sure they are paying attention. Listeners show they are paying attention by tilting their heads to one side, raising their eyebrows, nodding, and smiling every so often. When listeners disagree with the speaker, they may lean back and fold their arms across their chests. Some listeners may even shake their heads to show they disagree. When listeners are puzzled or confused by what the speaker is saying, they may frown or move their eyebrows together and squint their eyes.

You can tell from the body language of the people in this picture that they are interested in what is being said.

24

When speakers are in front of people in a public place, such as a classroom, they should pay attention to the kinds of body language their listeners are showing. If someone looks confused, the speaker can stop and ask if everyone understands. If people look bored, the speaker should change his or her **tone** of voice, change what he or she is doing (or the way it is being done), or take a break.

Know It

Listeners who are bored will look around, rest their heads on their hands or shoulders, and sometimes start to fall asleep.

The students in this classroom are not interested in the speaker, and their body language shows it.

25

You Can't Help It!

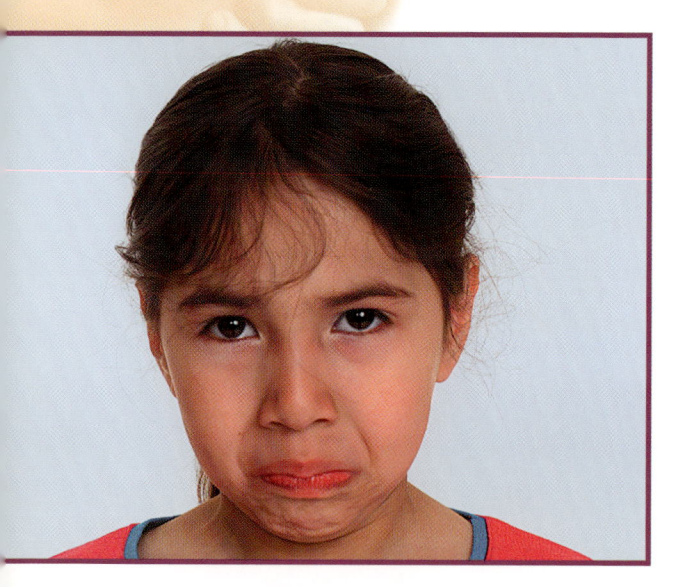

It is often difficult to keep tears from coming to your eyes when you feel sad.

When people are embarrassed, they can get red in the face. For some people, this does not happen as much when they get older.

Often people can control their **body language**. A bored person, for example, can try to sit up straight and look interested. A person who is worried about something can look as though everything is fine. There are some **emotions**, though, that are very hard to disguise because they affect our **autonomic nervous system**.

The autonomic nervous system controls organs such as the heart and stomach. It also causes **reactions** such as sweating, crying, **blushing**, and swallowing. If we are upset about something, we will probably have trouble keeping tears from coming into our eyes. One way people try to stop crying is to swallow a lot. This may help to stop the tears—but people will still be able to tell you are upset because you are swallowing so much.

The faces of some people turn bright red in certain situations. This redness is called blushing. It happens when the blood vessels in the face **dilate** and fill with blood. Usually a person's face, neck, and ears turn red when he or she blushes. Sometimes a person's whole body can tingle as well. People blush when they are embarrassed, angry, ashamed, or when they exercise.

The polygraph

The **polygraph** machine is also called a lie detector. People in **law enforcement** often use it to test whether someone is telling the truth. But how does it work?

When a person takes a polygraph test, the **examiner** places **sensors** on the person's body. The sensors record differences in autonomic nervous system responses. Three rubber tubes are wrapped around the person's chest to record breathing changes. Two small metal plates are put on the person's fingers to record sweating. A blood pressure cuff is put around the person's arm to record their heartbeat. These sensors are attached to a computer, which records the results of the test as it is given.

Next, the examiner asks a few questions to make sure the machine is working and that the person being tested is comfortable. Then the real test begins. The examiner asks questions, and the sensors record any change in breathing rate, heartbeat, and sweating. If the person's heart speeds up when a question is asked, the machine records the change. People who lie usually begin to breathe deeply. Their heartbeats speed up, and they begin to sweat. When these things happen, the pen records them on the paper. When the polygraph records a great change, it shows that the person has probably lied.

When some people get nervous or excited, they sweat. Sometimes people who feel guilty about something will sweat, too. They can sweat anywhere on their bodies, including their palms. They may also breathe heavily.

Autonomic nervous reactions are often embarrassing because they are very difficult, if not impossible, to control. Sometimes a person who blushes is embarrassed by blushing, making them blush even more!

Happy and Sad

These two women are obviously very happy. They both have wide smiles, their eyes are lit up, and they have a lot of energy.

Sadness is shown when the corners of the mouth turn down, as well as the eyes and the outsides of the eyebrows.

One of the things that is usually easiest to recognize from a person's **body language** is what he or she is feeling—his or her **emotions.** People's **posture, gestures, facial expressions,** and more show what they are feeling inside. Two of the easiest emotions to recognize are happiness and sadness.

The body language of a happy person is almost the opposite of the body language of a sad person. When people are happy, their eyes light up and sparkle. The sides of their mouths turn up, pushing the muscles in their cheeks up, too. People who are happy often have a lot of energy and interest in things around them. Sometimes happy people jump and dance around.

Maybe the reason we say we are "down" when we are sad is because that is what we look like. The muscles in our faces are in the "down" position. Our eyes turn down, and the corners of the mouth turn down. The outside edges of the eyebrows turn down, making the inside of the

28

You can see that these two children are very happy. The corners of their mouths are pointed up, their eyes are wide open, and their eyebrows are raised. They are probably jumping around, too.

eyebrows—the part closest to the nose—turn up. We often hang our heads and look down when we are sad, too. People who feel sad may not be very interested in what is happening around them. They often have low levels of energy and do not feel like doing much of anything.

Sometimes, changing your body language can change the way you feel inside. A person may be able to "trick" his or her body into feeling happy by doing "happy" things like smiling, laughing, and dancing. Even the small act of changing a frown into a smile moves different facial muscles and can release different chemicals inside the brain that may improve your mood. The next time you are having a bad day, try using "happy" body language on purpose. You just might feel better!

:-)	happy
:-(	sad
:*(	crying
X-(	mad
=8-0	surprised

Happy and sad on the Internet

When the Internet became a popular way to communicate, people discovered that it was difficult to express emotions. Part of the reason is that there is no way to show body language or use different voice qualities through e-mail. So, Internet users have developed a way of representing body language and facial expressions using "emoticons." These are symbols representing happiness, sadness, and a whole range of other emotions.

Fear and Relaxation

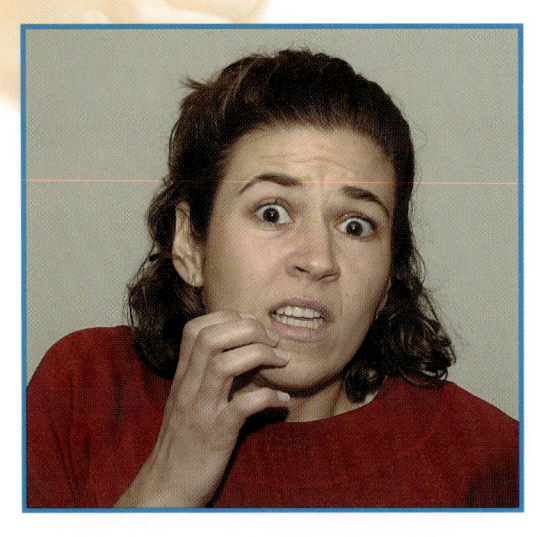

This woman has wide-open eyes and she has put her hand to her mouth. She is very frightened.

A comfortable sitting position, extended arms, and a calm **facial expression** show that this boy is relaxed.

Have you ever been startled or scared by something? How did it make you feel? You probably felt **tense,** or even nervous and uncomfortable. When you get a sudden scare, your brain sends a "red alert" message throughout your whole body. It releases chemicals that cause changes in your body, preparing you to deal with what is happening.

People who are suddenly frightened by something will have wide-open eyes. They may put their hands to their faces or over their mouths and scream. Their faces may turn red, and they may not be able to move for a moment. They will begin to breathe quickly and heavily, and may back away from the thing that scares them.

This kind of fear is actually fright, because it begins with some kind of shock. But your body can also show fear in other ways. Imagine, for example, that you hate to ride roller coasters that go upside down. But for some reason, you agree to wait in line with your friends to go on the ride anyway. As you get closer and closer to the front of the line, your

30

heart starts to pound. You may feel tingly, or even faint. As you step into the roller coaster car, you feel like you might be sick. When the car speeds down a hill and turns upside down, you close your eyes and grip the handlebar tightly. That is another way of showing fear.

On the other hand, people who are relaxed do not have as much trouble staying still. Their bodies are not tense, but comfortable. They sit in relaxed positions, often with their arms and legs extended. Relaxed people breathe easily and regularly, and they are quick to smile and laugh. In fact, **humor** is a good way to break any tension people may be feeling. Telling jokes or just being silly can put people at ease even in situations that seem difficult or uncomfortable. Laughter really can be "the best medicine"!

Know It

Your body's response to a sudden scare is sometimes called "fight or flight." Your body prepares either to face the situation ("fight") or to run away from it ("flight").

To tell the truth

Can you tell when someone is lying? Sometimes you can. If people are not telling the truth, they will often be nervous. They may not make **eye contact,** and they may **fidget** around. Dishonest people may sweat or **blush** as they lie. If they haven't prepared to tell the lie, they may say "um" and "uh" a lot. They will swallow more than normal, too.

If someone does these things, he or she may be lying. But some people work very hard to control their **body language** and facial expressions when they lie, so it is not always easy to tell.

Disgust and Surprise

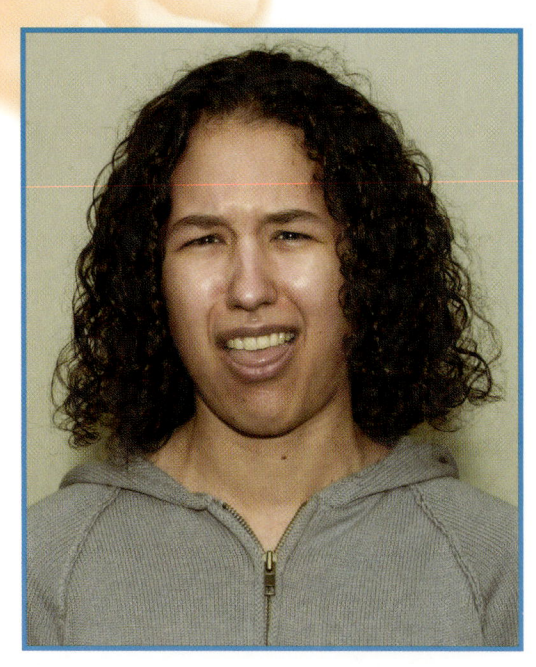

The typical expression for disgust includes lowered eyebrows, wrinkled eyes and nose, and a raised upper lip.

One common cause for disgust is food. But the same facial expression is used to communicate disgust in many different situations.

Everyone has at least one food they do not like to eat. Think of yours. What would you do if someone put a plate of it in front of you and said you had to eat it? You would most likely make a face. You might hold your nose or push the plate away. You might even start to feel sick. These are normal **reactions** when something disgusts you.

Your body may react with disgust to other things besides food. In fact, pretty much anything you dislike strongly can cause feelings of disgust. Some people react to bad smells. Others cannot stand the sight of blood. Many people are "grossed out" by the gory scenes in some horror movies. No matter what it is that disgusts people, they usually show it with almost the same kind of face. The nose wrinkles, and the upper lip goes up. The eyebrows are lowered as the eyes wrinkle.

Another **facial expression** that is common to almost everyone is surprise. Some surprises can be startling or scary. Other surprises that you might receive can be more pleasant. For example, imagine that it is your birthday. Your parents take you out for a nice dinner to celebrate. Then they tell you your best friend has asked that you stop by her house on your way home. You knock on the door of the house, and when your friend opens the door, you see lots of other people there yelling "Surprise!"

What kind of look would you have in this situation? Whether the surprise is pleasant or unpleasant, the first face you would make is basically the same. Your mouth would probably drop open, and your eyes would open wide. Then your body would try to decide quickly how it should react—with fear or with pleasure. In this case, you would probably feel comfortable with the situation. You might smile and look around to see who is at the party and what else is happening.

Acting

Imagine this: You found out about a big surprise party your friends are throwing for you, but you don't want anyone to know you found out. So when the door opens and everyone shouts "Surprise," you have to act surprised. Do you think you could make everyone believe that you were surprised?

That is what actors do. They try to imagine or remember what **emotions** feel like when they have to act them out. Then they use **body language** to act out the emotions, using facial expressions, **gestures,** and other movements. It is important for actors to know the different kinds of body language people use. This makes their acting more realistic. Some actors even study body language to learn all they can about it.

Your Emotions Are Showing!

The pictures on these pages show the **body language** of some **emotions**. Sometimes you can tell what a person is thinking or feeling just by looking at his or her face. Small clues like changes in the eyes or mouth can tell you all you need to know. Other times, you have to look at the entire body to "read" a person's body language.

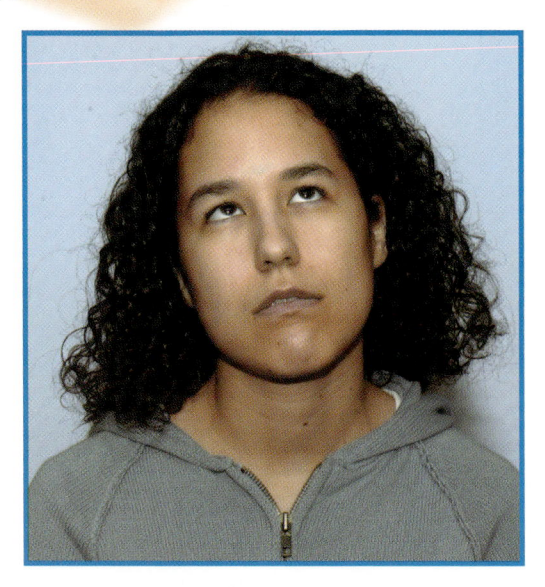

When people are frustrated, they often roll their eyes.

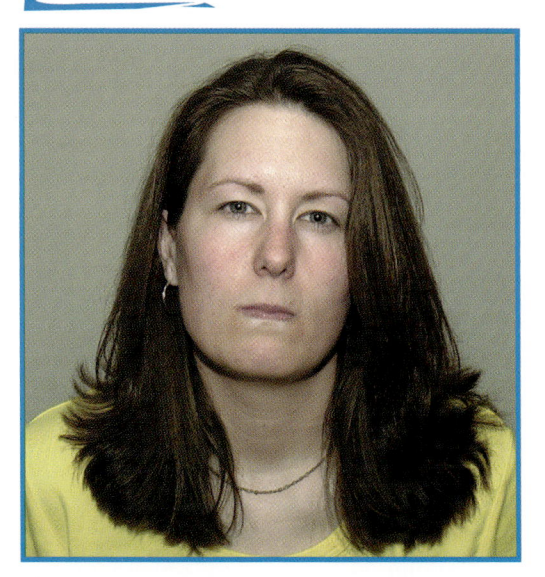

An angry person's lips often become thin. Also, their face may become red, tight, and **tense**.

When children don't get their own way, they often pout by thrusting out a lower lip. Adults do this sometimes, too.

The uniforms and baseball gloves tell us that these children are on a baseball team. Their body language says that they have probably just won a game.

As you look at the pictures, try to guess what the people might be thinking and feeling (without peeking at the captions first). What does their body language tell you? Also check the pictures for any clues that tell what might be happening to make the people think or feel the way they do. For example, the children in the picture above are wearing matching clothes and hats. They are holding baseball gloves, and they are in what looks like a park. What do these clues tell you about the children? If you combine this information with what the children's body language is showing, you can get a pretty good idea of what is happening. Can you make up a story about the picture? Compare your story with a friend's. Did the picture give you some of the same ideas?

You can also do this activity with pictures from other places, such as books or magazines. Use the body language and picture clues to make guesses about the pictures. A different game you can play to practice "reading" body language is an acting game. One person in a group chooses an emotion (see pages 42–43 for some ideas to get you started) and acts it out. The others in the group look at the body language being shown and try to guess the emotion.

Animals and Body Language

Animals also use **body language** to communicate with humans and other animals. If you have a pet, you probably know that it behaves in a certain way at certain times. Since we cannot communicate with our pets very well using words, it is helpful to understand their body language.

For example, cats have a certain body language when they are relaxed. The tail is down and the eyes look relaxed. When cats are excited and alert—for example, if they are ready to pounce on something, such as a mouse—their ears go forward and up, and their tail goes up. The pupils in their eyes **dilate,** and their back legs bend, ready to spring into action.

As the cat plays with a ball, its tail is up, and its ears are curled forward.

This cat's arched back and puffy tail tells us that it is feeling **threatened** by something in the room.

This dog's wagging tail and bright eyes show that it is very happy playing with the stick.

Pricked-up ears and a tilted head show that this dog has just heard something interesting.

When a cat feels threatened, it stands up straight and arches its back, trying to make itself look bigger and meaner than it really is. It will also fluff up the fur on its back and tail to look bigger. If the cat continues to feel threatened, it will begin hissing.

When people see a cat wagging its tail, they often think the cat is friendly because friendly dogs wag their tails. But when a cat waves its tail from side to side, it is not in a good mood. It will probably run away if you approach it. A stray cat wagging its tail may even claw at you if you try to pet it.

Dogs also use a great deal of body language. When a dog is afraid, its ears go back and its eyes narrow. The dog may start to tremble and whine, and its tail will go between its legs as it does when the dog is ashamed of something. On the other hand, a dog that is happy and feels playful will have happy-looking eyes and may pant with excitement. The dog may lower the front of its body to the ground. Happy dogs wag their tails and sometimes run around just for fun.

When a dog is on alert, such as when it hears a strange noise, its ears prick up. Sometimes the ears turn one way or another as the dog tries to hear a sound. The dog's tail may stand straight up, and its mouth will be closed.

People and animals

Some people love animals, and their body language around animals shows it. They will walk right up to all but the meanest-looking dog and pat its head or rub its ears. Other people, though, are uncomfortable or frightened around animals. They will back away if they see a dog or cat. If they are sitting down, they will lean away from the animal.

Body Language and Gestures Around the World

Many kinds of **body language** are acceptable all over the world. But some body language and **gestures** are considered rude in some parts of the world. And people in some **cultures** just do things differently from the way you may be used to.

Bulgaria
In Bulgaria, people nod their heads up and down to mean "no" and back and forth to mean "yes." This is the opposite of the way people do it in most of the world.

Germany
In Germany, you should not put your feet on furniture, no matter how comfortable it makes you feel!

France
In France, the **body language** for "ouch" is to hold the palms of your hands toward your body, open your fingers, and quickly shake your hands back and forth.

Japan
In Japan, it is rude to stand too close or to slap others on the back. People in Japan also smile when people from other countries would not, such as when they are sad, angry, or confused.

Lebanon

In Lebanon and many other countries, people stand closer together than they do in the United States and northern Europe.

Egypt

In many countries, including Egypt and other Arab nations, it is considered rude to sit with your legs crossed so that people can see the sole of your shoe.

Italy

Italians wave hello and goodbye differently than people in many other countries. They wave with their palm facing toward their bodies, not away from them.

Careers and Body Language

People who study **body language**, called **behaviorists**, have to study **psychology**, **anthropology**, and **sociology** in college. At work, they may conduct **experiments** that show how people act at different times. They write articles and books to help readers understand how people use body language. **Linguistic anthropologists** study the development of language over thousands of years, including body language.

The understanding and study of body language can be used in many other fields. Actors, for example, must study body language to be able to perform on the stage, in movies, and on television. Police officers and other people who work in **law enforcement** need to know about body language so they can tell when someone is lying or when someone is acting **suspiciously**. **Politicians** and people who are interested in public speaking need to know body language so they can see how an audience is **reacting** to what they are saying. They also use body

A knowledge of customer body language can be useful to salespeople in many different industries.

People who speak in front of large crowds often use large **gestures** to communicate their ideas.

40

People who coach athletes should know how to read the body language of their own players and of the players on the opposing team. This may help the coaches figure out how to win the game.

language when they speak so they can get their point across to the audience. Salespeople study body language to see whether a customer needs help or is ready to make a purchase. They will use different **tactics** depending on the customer's body language. Teachers need to understand the body language of students so they can tell whether the class understands what they are teaching. Writers need to know about body language to make the **behavior** of their characters seem realistic. Artists who know about body language will draw, paint, and **sculpt** people whose **emotions** are obvious.

Understanding why people act the way they do is important in every job. Knowing about body language can make anyone's work easier because it tells us what people are thinking and what is behind their behavior.

Appendix A: Common Emotions and Body Language Signs

The number of **emotions** that can be expressed by the human body is very large. To make a complete dictionary of all of the emotions and their corresponding **body language**, you would need hundreds of pages. The following are photographs of some of the most common emotions. Each photograph is labeled with the emotion it is showing, as well as a description of the expressions and **gestures** used to communicate that emotion.

Anger
Anger is expressed with a red face, the mouth set in a tight line (lips may be thin), squinting eyes, and lowered eyebrows.

Stubbornness
This **emotion** is shown by arms crossed over the chest, legs in a closed position, staring eyes, and the mouth in a tight line.

Fear
People express fear with wide-open eyes, hands near the face as if to defend, and an open mouth.

Happiness
People are happy when they laugh, smile with their teeth showing, and their eyes have wrinkles around them.

Sadness
Sadness is expressed by looking downward, crying, and lowering the eyes and the corners of the mouth.

Embarrassment
An embarrassed person will laugh nervously, avoid **eye contact**, turn away, and **blush**.

Disbelief
Disbelief is expressed when someone rolls their eyes, shakes their head, and breathes out through clenched teeth.

Appendix B: Common Gestures

The following **gestures** are listed with their common meanings in the United States. Remember that these same gestures and expressions can have different meanings in different **cultures.**

Hat tip
greeting done by briefly touching the brim of the hat

Hat raise
greeting done by quickly removing hat and putting it back on

Pointing index finger
pointing out something; can be rude if pointing at a person

"High-five"
palms raised and slapped together; indicates congratulations

"Knock on wood"
done to ensure protection

Moving fingers up and down in a "talking" motion
means someone talks too much

Patting belly
shows "I am full"

Index finger beckon
means "come here"

Fanning face with hand
means "I am hot"

More Books to Read

George, Jean Craighead. *How to Talk to Your Dog.* New York: HarperCollins Publishers, 2000.

Kaner, Etta. *Animals Talk: How Animals Communicate Through Sight, Sound and Smell.* Buffalo, N.Y.: Kids Can Press, 2002.

Robson, Pam. *Body Language.* Danbury, Conn.: Scholastic Library Publishing, 1998.

Sanders, Pete, and Steve Myers. *Love, Hate and Other Feelings.* Brookfield, Conn.: Millbrook Press, Incorporated, 2000.

Glossary

anchor in television, person who reads the news or hosts a program

anthropology study of human beings

anxiety strong feeling of worry

authority power or control over another person

autonomic nervous system nerves that control heartbeat, sweating, and other actions

barrier something in the way; a block

behavior person's actions and reactions

behaviorist person who studies behavior

blush turn red

body language body movements that send a message; movements can include facial expressions, eye contact, and posture

confident feeling sure of one's self; good feeling that you can do something well

culture beliefs and behaviors of a particular group of people

dilate get bigger

diplomat person in a government who deals with other countries

emotion deep feeling; anger, sorrow, and joy are emotions

examiner person in charge of giving a test

experiment test done to see whether something is true

expressive showing much emotion or feeling

eye contact direct look into another person's eyes

facial expression way the face looks when a person feels a certain way; expressions can show sadness, happiness, fear, and many other emotions

fidget make nervous movements

gesture nonverbal signs used and understood by many people

humor something funny or amusing

illustrator hand movements used to help explain speech

kinesics study of body movements and how they communicate a message

law enforcement people who keep the law; includes police officers, state troopers, sheriff's deputies

linguistic anthropologist person who studies the development of language

nonverbal communication communication using something other than speech

official business business done for the state or government

pace speed

pitch level of voice; a high voice is said to have a high pitch, and a low voice has a low pitch

politician person in government, or who wishes to be in government

polygraph instrument that records changes in the human body; used to tell if a person is lying

posture way someone holds their body; standing and sitting up straight is good posture

proxemics study of personal distance, or the spaces humans keep between themselves and others

psychology science of the mind and behavior

react respond to something

royalty people to whom society has given a special place, usually by birth; kings and queens are royalty

sculpt to carve and make a statue or other artwork from something solid, such as marble or wood

sensor device that can measure changes in a person's body

shriek high-pitched cry or shout

society group of people who live in a certain place, such as a country, and have ways of living and behavior in common

sociology study of society

suspiciously when someone behaves in an unusual way that suggests they are doing something wrong

tactic step taken with a certain goal in mind

tense feeling that results from stress and pressure; when people feel tense, they often get headaches or muscle aches

threaten make someone feel as if they are going to be hurt in some way

tone way the voice expresses a feeling or emotion

universally known by all people

verbal using spoken words

violate break an accepted rule

volume measurement of loudness

Index

actors 33, 40
animals 36–37
anthropology 40
artists 11, 41
autonomic nervous system 26, 27

behavior 4, 41
behaviorist 4, 5, 11, 20, 22, 23, 40
blushing 26, 27, 31, 43
Bulgaria 38

classroom 5, 25
cultures 7, 10, 14, 20, 21, 22, 23, 38, 44

da Vinci, Leonardo 11
diplomats 21

Egypt 39
emoticons 29
emotions
   angry 7, 17, 18, 19, 26, 34, 38, 42
   bored 5, 12, 13, 20, 25, 26
   confident 17, 8
   confused 6, 19, 24, 25, 38
   disbelief 6, 43
   disgusted 32
   excited 4, 13, 18, 19, 27, 36, 37
   fear 6, 10, 30–31, 33, 42
   frustrated 6, 17, 34
   happy 6, 7, 10, 11, 13, 28–29, 36, 37, 43
   nervous 19, 27, 30, 31, 43
   puzzled 24
   relaxed 10, 12, 19, 30–31, 36
   sad 6, 8, 9, 10, 13, 26, 28–29, 38, 43
   scared 13, 30–31, 32
   surprised 6, 7, 10, 29, 32–33
   tense 23, 30, 31, 34
   worried 10, 26

Ethiopia 20
exercises 7
eye contact 8–9, 31, 43
eyebrows 7, 24, 28, 29, 32, 42

facial expressions 11, 28, 29, 30, 31, 32
France 21, 22, 38
frown 7, 10, 24, 29

game 35
Germany 38
gestures 13, 16, 17, 20–21, 28, 33, 38–39, 40, 42–43
Great Britain 14, 17, 20, 22

hands 5, 12, 13, 16–17, 20, 21, 23, 25, 30, 38, 42, 44
handshake 17
hips 13, 17

illustrator 16
Italy 11, 20, 21, 39

Japan 21, 39

kinesics 4

law enforcement 27, 40
Lebanon 39
linguistic anthropologists 40
listening 5, 7, 13, 24–25
lying 9, 31, 40

Mona Lisa 11
mouth 4, 7, 11, 10–11, 28, 30, 33, 34, 37, 42

Netherlands 21
northern Europe 14, 39

pace 18, 19
palms 17, 20, 27, 38, 44
pets 36–37
pitch 18, 19
polygraph 27

posture 12–13, 28
pout 34
proxemics 14–15
psychology 40
Puerto Rico 22

reactions 6, 26, 27, 32
reading body language 11, 24, 34–35, 41
royalty 20

salespeople 40, 41
Saudi Arabia 21
signals 5, 6, 7, 24
smile 4, 7, 10–11, 28, 29, 31, 33, 38, 43
sociology 40
speaking 4, 5, 7, 8, 9, 18–19, 24–25, 40
strangers 8, 13, 14, 15, 22, 23
swallowing 26, 31
sweating 26, 27, 31

tone 18, 19, 25
touch 22–23

United States 14, 17, 20, 22, 39, 44

voice 18–19, 25
volume 18, 19

48